# Confederation Bridge

## Simon Rose

Weigl

Published by Weigl Educational Publishers Limited
6325 10th Street SE
Calgary, Alberta T2H 2Z9

Website: www.weigl.ca

Library and Archives Canada Cataloguing in Publication

Rose, Simon, 1961-
    Confederation Bridge / Simon Rose.
(Canadian virtual field trip)
Includes index.
ISBN 978-1-77071-481-6 (bound).--ISBN 978-1-77071-484-7 (pbk.)
    1. Confederation Bridge (N.B. and P.E.I.)--Juvenile literature.
I. Title.  II. Series: Canadian virtual field trip series

TG27.N67R67 2012          j388.1'3209717          C2011-908213-6

Printed in the United States of America in North Mankato, Minnesota
1 2 3 4 5 6 7 8 9 0  16 15 14 13 12

072012
WEP250612

Editor: Heather Kissock
Design: Terry Paulhus

Every reasonable effort has been made to trace ownership and to obtain permission to reprint copyright material. The publishers would be pleased to have any errors or omissions brought to their attention so that they may be corrected in subsequent printings.

Weigl acknowledges Getty Images as its primary image supplier for this title.

We acknowledge the financial support of the Government of Canada through the Canada Book Fund for our publishing activities.

# Contents

# What is the Confederation Bridge?

Spanning across the Northumberland Strait, **Confederation** Bridge connects the eastern Canadian provinces of Prince Edward Island and New Brunswick. The two-lane highway toll bridge joins Borden-Carleton in Prince Edward Island with Cape Jourimain in New Brunswick. While not the longest bridge in the world, it is the world's longest bridge that crosses ice-covered water.

The Confederation Bridge is one of Canada's greatest **engineering** achievements. It has greatly simplified travel in Atlantic Canada, making the trip between the two provinces much more convenient for both visitors and residents. Before the bridge was built, most travellers had to make the crossing on a **ferry**, which took about 75 minutes. The bridge crossing now takes only 10 minutes by vehicle.

The naming of the bridge was opened to the Canadian public. Approximately 2,200 suggestions were received. After narrowing the list down to three possibilities, the name Confederation Bridge was announced on September 27, 1996. The name has links to Canada's past and also indicates the joining of the two provinces.

Before Confederation Bridge received its official name, the people living on Prince Edward Island often called it "the fixed link."

# Snapshot of Prince Edward Island

Prince Edward Island (PEI) is one of Canada's Maritime Provinces. Located in the Gulf of St. Lawrence, it is Canada's smallest province, in both size and population. The province of Nova Scotia lies to its south. To its west is New Brunswick.

## INTRODUCING PEI

**CAPITAL CITY:** Charlottetown

**FLAG:**

**MOTTO:** *Parva sub ingenti*
(The small under the protection of the great)

**POPULATION:** 145,855 (2011)

**JOINED CONFEDERATION:** July 1, 1873

**CLIMATE:** Warm summers with moderately cold winters

**SUMMER TEMPERATURE:** Average of 23° Celsius

**WINTER TEMPERATURE:** Average of −3°C

**TIME ZONE:** Atlantic Standard Time (AST)

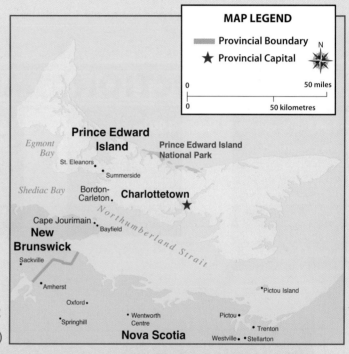

MAP LEGEND
- Provincial Boundary
- ★ Provincial Capital

0 — 50 miles
0 — 50 kilometres

Egmont Bay
Prince Edward Island
Prince Edward Island National Park
St. Eleanors
Summerside
Shediac Bay
Bordon-Carleton
Charlottetown
Cape Jourimain
New Brunswick
Bayfield
Sackville
Northumberland Strait
Amherst
Pictou Island
Oxford
Wentworth Centre
Pictou
Springhill
Trenton
Westville · Stellarton
Nova Scotia

## PEI Symbols

Prince Edward Island has several official symbols. Some symbols represent the features that distinguish the area from other parts of Canada. Others indicate the unique place PEI has in the history of the country.

COAT OF ARMS

**PROVINCIAL FLOWER**
Lady's Slipper

**PROVINCIAL TREE**
Northern Red Oak

**PROVINCIAL BIRD**
Blue Jay

# A Step Back in Time

When Prince Edward Island officially joined Canada in 1873, the federal government promised to provide connections to the mainland. The plan was to provide a passenger boat that would link people to the rapidly developing Canadian railway system. Early efforts, however, did not go as planned. In winter, ice in the Northumberland Strait prevented ships from passing through. Over time, new ships, capable of breaking through the ice, were built. Ferries began crossing the strait in 1938. The ferries had a special deck for cars.

## CONSTRUCTION TIMELINE

**1992**
On December 2, the Canadian government announces that the bridge's construction will finally begin.

**1993**
Construction crews begin setting up their equipment in the fall.

**1994 to 1996**
Bridge parts are manufactured in staging yards on each side of the strait.

**1994 to 1997**
Workers begin placing the components that will form the bridge.

Cranes were shipped out to the construction site to help place the bridge's pieces together.

A fixed link across the Northumberland Strait had been discussed as far back as the 1870s. It was not until 1987, however, that the Canadian government finally approved the building of a bridge. A **plebiscite** was held on January 18, 1988, to let the people of PEI make the final decision as to whether or not the bridge could go ahead. At 59.4 percent, the "Yes" vote won.

Ferries are still available for people wanting a more leisurely ride across the strait.

**August 1996**
The piece marking the bridge's halfway point is put in place by crane.

**November 1996**
The main structure of the bridge is completed on November 19.

**1997**
**Approach roads**, toll booths, and other finishing touches are completed.

**1997**
The bridge is officially opened on May 31.

By October 1996, the bridge almost reached Prince Edward Island.

# The Confederation Bridge's Location

The Confederation Bridge spans the Northumberland Strait at Abegweit Passage. This is the narrowest point of the strait. The bridge is part of the Trans-Canada Highway. It connects the western shore of PEI and the southeastern tip of New Brunswick.

Abegweit is a Mi'kmaq nickname for Prince Edward Island. Abegweit comes from the Mi'kmaq language, meaning "cradled on the waves."

# The Confederation Bridge Today

The Confederation Bridge is open year-round, 24 hours a day. As a result of the bridge being built, the number of visitors to Prince Edward Island jumped from 740,000 in 1996 to 1.2 million in 1997. The island now receives about 900,000 tourists each year. The rise in tourism on Prince Edward Island has made new opportunities for restaurants, stores, and other businesses.

**Width** From guardrail to guardrail, the bridge is 11 metres wide.

**Length** The bridge is 12.9 kilometres long.

12.9 kilometres

**Piers** Sixty-five **piers** hold up the bridge's roadway.

# The Structure of the Bridge

*The Confederation Bridge is made up of several structural components. Each component helps to make the bridge strong.*

**West Approach Bridge** The Confederation Bridge has three distinct sections. The West Approach Bridge is the section of the bridge that leaves New Brunswick's Cape Jourimain. It is 1.3 kilometres long and is supported by 14 piers.

An approach bridge is a section of bridge that links the land to the section that goes over the obstacle for which the bridge was built.

The Navigation Span is high enough for some cruise ships to sail underneath.

**Main Bridge** The Main Bridge is the section that extends over the waters of the Northumberland Strait. It is connected to the two approach bridges. The Main Bridge is 11 kilometres long and is supported by 44 piers. This part of the bridge contains a section called the Navigation Span. This is an elevated section under which large ships can travel.

Gateway Village is located at the foot of the East Approach Bridge. The village consists of a visitor centre and railway museum, as well as several restaurants and shops.

**East Approach Bridge** The East Approach Bridge leaves the town of Borden-Carleton in Prince Edward Island. It is supported by seven piers and extends for 0.6 kilometres.

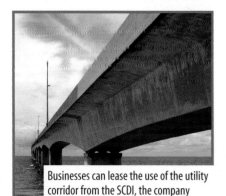
Businesses can lease the use of the utility corridor from the SCDI, the company responsible for operating the bridge.

**Utility Corridor** The Confederation Bridge has a hollow interior core called the utility corridor. Cables and wiring extend from one end of the corridor to the other. These cables and wiring send electricity, telephone services, and other utilities to and from Prince Edward Island.

The safety barrier wall blocks most of the view from the bridge. This helps drivers keep their eyes on the road.

**Roadway** The Confederation Bridge has a two-lane highway with emergency lanes on each side. A 1.1-metre safety barrier runs along the side of the road to ensure vehicles stay on the bridge. The roadway sits on concrete **box girders** that are connected to the top of the piers. The girders follow the path of the roadway, providing the support it needs. The roadway itself has a **bituminous** mixture over it that reduces vehicle spray during wet weather.

**Piers** The piers are the structures on which the bridge's roadway sits. Each **shaft** of the Confederation Bridge's 65 piers is octagonal, or eight-sided, and hollow. The base of each pier's shaft is cemented to the **bedrock** on the ocean floor for stability. Each base has a cone-shaped shield attached to protect it from ice in the winter.

The bridge's piers have been placed 250 metres apart from each other.

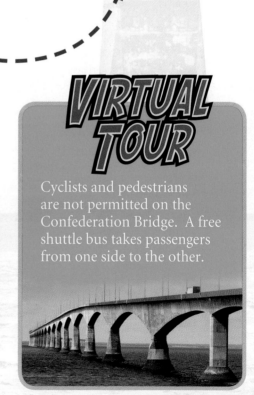

### VIRTUAL TOUR

Cyclists and pedestrians are not permitted on the Confederation Bridge. A free shuttle bus takes passengers from one side to the other.

# Features of the Bridge

*The Confederation Bridge has a number of features that ensure the safety of those who use it.*

**Bridge Control Centre** The Bridge Control Centre is located on the PEI side of the bridge. The centre is staffed 24 hours a day. Staff monitor traffic flow and weather. They also watch for any situations on the bridge that could affect user safety, such as accidents or fog. If any situations arise, the staff take the necessary steps to bring them under control.

The Bridge Control Centre is located in Gateway Village.

**Toll Booths** There is only one toll station for the Confederation Bridge. It is located on the PEI side of the bridge. People pay the toll only when they are leaving the island. The station consists of seven toll booths, including one self-serve lane for people using credit and debit cards. Foot passengers and cyclists pay their toll inside the main facility.

Even though using the bridge costs money, it is still considered the least expensive way to cross the Northumberland Strait.

## Weather Monitoring

The Confederation Bridge has its own weather station that keeps track of wind speed and direction, precipitation levels, and road and air temperature. This is done using sensors that are located along the bridge. Station employees use this information to determine whether the bridge is safe for driving. They may lower the speed limit or halt traffic completely if conditions are not safe.

Ice formation is considered one of the major hazards on the bridge.

Electronic signage provides drivers on the bridge with information about driving conditions.

**Emergency Services** The bridge features 22 television cameras that monitor driving conditions and traffic flow 24 hours a day. This information is fed back to the management centre for review. To help drivers respond quickly to problems, emergency telephones and fire extinguishers are positioned along the bridge every 750 metres.

**Electrical Systems** The bridge is equipped with its own power supply as well as a back-up generator in case of a blackout. The electrical system is responsible for the operation of the bridge's 310 street lights and 17 traffic lights. Beside each traffic light is an electronic sign that posts the speed limit. The speed limit can be changed by the control centre in the event of a change in driving conditions.

When driving conditions on the bridge are normal, all lights are green.

# Big Ideas Behind the Bridge

There were many issues to take into consideration when planning the Confederation Bridge. Builders had to determine what kind of bridge would work best and how to prepare the parts that would make up the bridge.

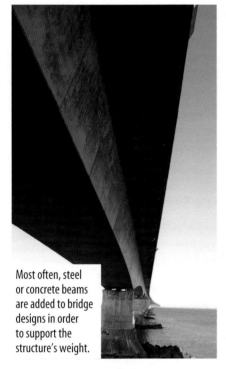

Most often, steel or concrete beams are added to bridge designs in order to support the structure's weight.

## Tension and Compression

As bridges span greater distances, the forces acting on them increase. **Compression** and **tension** are two forces that builders face. On a bridge, excess compression can cause the surface to buckle, and excess tension can cause it to snap. To avoid these problems, bridge designers spread the pressure out over a large area. The Confederation Bridge is a beam bridge. It consists of a long, solid beam that is supported by columns. Pressure, such as traffic travelling across the bridge, is supported by columns. On a beam bridge, compression acts on the top side of the beam, causing it to shorten in width. This creates tension on the lower part of the beam, causing it to lengthen. To correct the forces of compression and tension, bridge designers increase the width of the beam.

## Precast Concrete

Confederation Bridge is made mostly of concrete, a substance that can be shaped into any form. Liquid concrete is allowed to harden inside containers called casts. The concrete takes on the shape of the cast as it hardens. Sometimes, concrete is poured into its cast on the construction site. In some cases, however, it is poured into its cast at a different location and then shipped to the job site. When this is done, the cast is called precast. The concrete for the Confederation Bridge was precast.

The concrete was cast at staging facilities in Bayfield, New Brunswick, and Borden-Carleton, PEI. A monument to the builders now stands in Borden-Carleton.

# Science at Work at the Bridge

A special crane called the Svanen was used to assemble the pieces of Confederation Bridge in Northumberland Strait. The crane was built specifically for building on water. It relied on science to do its job.

The Svanen was capable of lifting 8,700 tonnes.

## Buoyancy

As the bridge had to be put together in the water, boats played a key role in its construction. Boats are buoyant, which means they float in liquid. This is because the force of the water pushing up on the boat is greater than the force pushing down. The floating crane sat on top of a catamaran. This is a **twin-hulled** boat. Due to their design, twin hulls give a boat more stability in the water. Floating cranes need this stability because they are balancing their weight, as well as the weight of the objects they are lifting.

## Pulleys

A pulley is a wheel with a grooved rim through which a cable or chain is guided. Pulleys help raise and lower heavy **loads** by changing the direction of a pulling force. Pulling on one side of the cable causes the wheel to turn. This moves the other end of the cable in the opposite direction. Cranes are machines that lift and move heavy construction materials. They use pulleys to operate. The crane for the Confederation Bridge was used to lift and place the concrete beams and piers into their proper position.

Pulling down on one side of the pulley lifts an object on the other side.

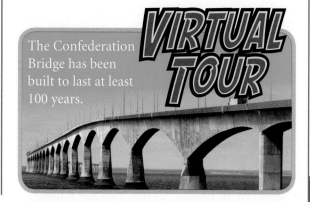

The Confederation Bridge has been built to last at least 100 years.

# The Bridge's Builders

Building a bridge the size and scale of Confederation Bridge takes careful planning and special skills. It also requires hard work. Architects and engineers worked together to design the bridge, while construction workers and labourers assembled the bridge piece by piece.

Jean Muller helped design the Seven-Mile Bridge in the Florida Keys of the United States. The bridge is actually 6.79 miles (10.93 kilometres) long.

### Jean Muller Designer and Engineer

Jean Muller was the chief designer and engineer of the Confederation Bridge. Born in France in 1925, he received his initial training at L'École Centrale des Arts et Manufactures in Paris. After leaving school, he began working under Eugène Freyssinet, a well-known and respected engineer. From Freyssinet, Muller learned about the techniques involved in building concrete bridges. Over the course of his career, Muller became known for inventing new bridge-building techniques. Besides Confederation Bridge, he is also known for designing the Oléron Bridge in France, Switzerland's Chillon **Viaduct**, and the Seven Mile Bridge in the Florida Keys.

### Stantec Engineers

Stantec is an engineering firm located in Edmonton, Alberta. It worked with Jean Muller on the construction of the Confederation Bridge. The company helped make sure the bridge was structurally sound. Founded in 1954, the company has become an industry leader in **sustainable** building techniques. The Confederation Bridge is just one of the many projects it has helped create. The company is also responsible for redesigning the Peace River Bridge on the Alaska Highway and the expansion of the Snowbasin Resort in Salt Lake City, Utah, in preparation for the 2002 Winter Olympics.

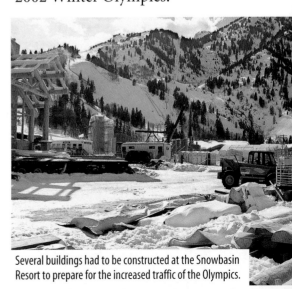

Several buildings had to be constructed at the Snowbasin Resort to prepare for the increased traffic of the Olympics.

## Structural Engineers

Structural engineers communicate closely with architects, other engineers, and construction contractors to ensure the safety and stability of the structure being built.

Structural engineers study a structure's design and determine how to make the design a reality. Their job relies mainly on a knowledge of scientific principles involved in carrying loads. The structural engineer makes sure the structure will hold together under its weight and the weight it is designed to bear, such as cars, trucks, and trailers. Structural engineers conduct tests at different stages of the construction process. They ensure that the structure will be able to withstand wind, rain, vibration, and other forces once it is complete.

## Concrete Finishers

Construction workers that specialize in concrete are called concrete finishers. Concrete finishers pour wet concrete into casts and spread it to a desired thickness. They level and smooth the surface and edges of the concrete. Concrete finishers also repair, waterproof, and restore concrete surfaces. Concrete finishers must know how to age or cure concrete perfectly in order for this construction material to have maximum strength.

Concrete finishing is very physical work. Workers in this field are constantly bending, stooping, kneeling, and lifting heavy bags of cement.

## Labourers

Labourers are an important part of any construction team.

Labourers play a key role at any construction site. They get the materials into the hands of the people who need them. They do this by carrying the materials on their shoulders, carting them in wheelbarrows, and loading them onto trucks and other vehicles. Labourers help keep job sites clean. They know how to use tools, such as saws and hammers, and can operate a variety of construction equipment.

# Similar Structures Around the World

Bridges come in a variety of shapes and sizes. They are made from a range of materials. All of them serve the important function of getting people and products over physical obstacles that include rivers, lakes, and valleys.

## Danyang-Kunshan Grand Bridge

**BUILT:** 2011
**LOCATION:** Jiangsu Province, China
**DESIGN:** China High Speed Railways
**DESCRIPTION:** The Danyang–Kunshan Grand Bridge is a 164-kilometre long viaduct on the Beijing to Shanghai High Speed Railway. It is currently the world's longest bridge. A 9-kilometre stretch of the bridge is over water, crossing Yangcheng Lake. Construction of the bridge, which employed 10,000 people, took four years and cost about $8.5 billion.

More than 42,000 vehicles cross the Lake Pontchartrain Causeway every weekday.

Trains travelling on the Beijing-Shanghai High Speed Railway can reach speeds of 380 kilometres per hour. The trip between Beijing and Shanghai can be completed in less than five hours.

## Lake Pontchartrain Causeway

**BUILT:** 1969
**LOCATION:** Louisiana, USA
**DESIGN:** Palmer and Baker Inc.
**DESCRIPTION:** The **causeway** is made up of two parallel bridges crossing Lake Pontchartrain in southern Louisiana. The bridges are supported by 9,500 concrete **piles**. The longer of the two bridges is 38.35 kilometres long. From 1969, it was officially the world's longest bridge over water. This changed, however, in 2011, with the building of the 42.5-kilometre long Jiaozhou Bay Bridge in China.

## King Fahd Causeway

**BUILT:** 1986
**LOCATION:** Saudi Arabia and Bahrain
**DESIGN:** Ballast Nedam
**DESCRIPTION:** The King Fahd Causeway is a four-lane road connecting Bahrain and Saudi Arabia. Surveys began in 1968, and construction took place between 1981 and 1986. The causeway is approximately 23 metres wide and is 25.8 kilometres long. It was built using more than 45,000 tonnes of reinforced steel and 353,032 square metres of concrete, at a cost of about $1.2 billion.

The King Fahd Causeway is the only land link Bahrain has with the outside world.

## Vasco da Gama Bridge

**BUILT:** 1998
**LOCATION:** Tagus River, Portugal
**DESIGN:** Armando Rito
**DESCRIPTION:** The Vasco da Gama Bridge, crossing the Tagus River near Lisbon, has viaducts and a cable-stayed design. It is the longest bridge in Europe, with a total length of 17.2 kilometres, including 0.8 kilometres for the main bridge, 11.4 kilometres in viaducts, and 4.8 kilometres in access roads. The bridge opened to commemorate Expo 98, a World's Fair marking Vasco da Gama's discovery of the sea route from Western Europe to India in 1498.

Due to the proposed length of the Vasco da Gama Bridge, engineers had to factor in the curvature of Earth during the design process.

# Issues Facing the Confederation Bridge

The Confederation Bridge is a strong, impressive structure. However, there are dangers that can make it vulnerable to damage and destruction.

## WHAT IS THE ISSUE?

| | | |
|---|---|---|
| The area experiences Canadian winters. Ice is present in the Northumberland Strait for five months every year. | High winds are common in open areas such as the Northumberland Strait. | Drivers tend to lose concentration on long stretches of straight road. |

## EFFECTS

| | | |
|---|---|---|
| Ice and slush can form on the road surface, making driving conditions hazardous. | High winds can be a danger to vehicles crossing the bridge. Large gusts can push motorcycles, trucks, and other high-sided vehicles into the wrong lane. | Drivers who are not paying attention are more likely to cause traffic collisions. |

## ACTION TAKEN

| | | |
|---|---|---|
| The bridge has more than 7,000 drainage ports. These ports allow slush and water to safely run off the sides of the bridge. | Confederation Bridge Control monitors wind speeds 24 hours a day. When steady winds exceed 69 kilometres per hour, restrictions are placed on at-risk vehicles. | The Confederation Bridge was designed with curves to ensure that drivers remain attentive while crossing. |

# Build a Bridge

Anyone can build a basic bridge. If you have ever placed a plank of wood across a stream so you could cross without getting wet, you have built a bridge. However, bridges that support thousands of cars or people are much more complicated to build.

Try building the bridge below and see how much weight it can hold.

## Materials
• box of toothpicks
• bag of mini-marshmallows
• popsicle sticks
• glue

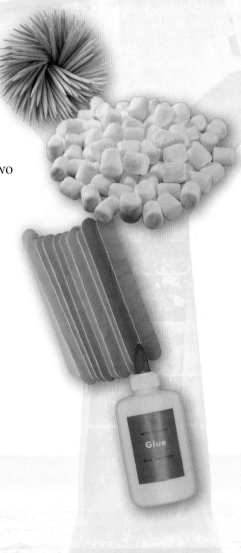

## Instructions
1. Poke a toothpick halfway through the sides of two marshmallows. Then, poke another toothpick halfway through the top of each marshmallow. Poke the other ends of the toothpicks into another marshmallow. This forms a triangle with a marshmallow at each point.

2. Continue connecting toothpicks and marshmallows until you have three triangles. These will make up one side of the bridge.

3. Repeat this process to build the other side of the bridge.

4. Place one side flat on the table. Then, place toothpicks through each corner of the triangles. Connect the other side of the bridge to these toothpicks. This completes the frame of the bridge.

5. To build the roadway, glue popsicle sticks to the bottom section of the bridge. Test the strength of the bridge with items from around your house.

# Confederation Bridge Quiz

**Q** How many piers does the main part of the Confederation Bridge rest on?

**A** 44

**Q** What percentage of Prince Edward Islanders voted in favour of a fixed link in 1988?

**A** 59.4 percent

**Q** How long is the Confederation Bridge?

**A** 12.9 kilometres

**Q** What body of water does the Confederation Bridge cross?

**A** The Northumberland Strait

# Further Research

You can find more information about Confederation Bridge, its features, and its history at your local library or on the internet.

For more information about travelling over Confederation Bridge, go to **www.confederationbridge.com**

Learn more about the connection between Confederation Bridge and the Trans-Canada Highway at **www.transcanadahighway.com/pei/info-confederationbridge.htm**

Read about how the Svanen crane helped in the construction of Confederation Bridge at **www.thecanadianencyclopedia.com/articles/macleans/peis-engineering-marvel**

# Glossary

**approach roads:** roadways that take people and vehicles to a structure

**bedrock:** the solid rock that underlies loose material, such as soil, sand, clay, or gravel

**bituminous:** containing a black, oily substance that comes from decomposed organic matter

**box girders:** support beams that are hollow and square or rectangular in shape

**causeway:** a raised road, usually over a body of water and often constructed from landfill or piles of rocks

**compression:** the act of being flattened or squeezed together by pressure

**Confederation:** the uniting of several provinces or territories into one country, such as the Confederation of Canada in 1867

**engineering:** the branch of science and technology concerned with the design, building, and use of engines, machines, and structures

**ferry:** a vessel travelling on water between two points, often linking an island to the mainland

**loads:** weights or sources of pressure carried by an object

**piers:** concrete pillars sunk into the sea or riverbed so that the main bridge sections can rest on top of them

**piles:** columns that are driven into the ground to support a vertical load

**plebiscite:** a vote made by the people outside of normal election time

**shaft:** the middle part of a column

**sustainable:** capable of long-term use without harm to the environment

**tension:** the pulling force exerted on an object

**twin-hulled:** having two parallel floats

**viaduct:** a bridge consisting of a set of arches supported by a row of piers or towers

# Index